SAINT ANDREW

Patron Saint of Scotland

Lois Rock

Illustrated by Finola Stack

LION
CHILDREN'S

Who Was Andrew?

Andrew was one of Jesus' disciples. The Gospel of John, in the Bible, says he was the first person to follow Jesus. He was so convinced Jesus was the Son of God that he brought his brother, Simon, to meet him, and Simon became a trusted follower too.

Jesus' disciples saw their master put to death on a cross, but soon they were travelling to many different places telling everyone that Jesus was alive again and that they should listen to the things he had taught. According to ancient writings, Andrew went to Greece and Asia Minor and what he said convinced many other people to become followers of Jesus. For this, Andrew was put to death by order of a Roman ruler.

Andrew's link with Scotland came much later. One story is that in 345 a monk named Regulus

(sometimes called Rule)
was told by an angel to
take the remains of
Andrew – and the
news about Jesus –
to the ends of the
earth. Scotland was
the furthest place
Regulus could reach.

This stained-
glass picture
of Andrew shows
him holding the
X-shaped cross
on which he
was crucified.

Andrew: Fisherman for Jesus

NDREW HAD TAKEN the day off fishing. He wanted to go to see the preacher everyone was talking about, John the Baptist.

'Get ready for God,' said John. 'Live your lives as God wants. If you are prepared to be baptized, I will baptize you here in the River Jordan.'

Andrew was among the many who trusted the words of John the Baptist.

Not long after, John pointed out another man to his followers. 'Look,' said John. 'When I baptized him, I saw the Spirit of God come down from heaven like a dove. He is the Son of God.'

Andrew and a friend got up and followed the man. They wanted to listen to all he had to teach them.

Andrew was thrilled with what he heard. He rushed to fetch his brother, Simon. 'We have found the

6

Messiah,' he exclaimed. 'His name is Jesus, and he truly is God's special king.'

Simon went with Andrew, and Jesus knew at once that he had found another loyal follower. 'Your name is Simon,' he said, 'but I will call you Peter.' It was a nickname, meaning 'a rock'.

The days went by. More and more people came to listen to Jesus. They believed what he said about living in the way that pleased God – as part of God's kingdom – and wanted to be his followers. When Jesus chose a band of twelve to be his special helpers in spreading the message, Andrew and Simon Peter were among them.

One day, 5,000 people gathered to listen to Jesus. As evening came, Jesus told the twelve to find food for the crowd. 'But that will cost an enormous amount of money,' said one. 'And there's nowhere we could buy anything anyway.'

Andrew had an idea. 'There is a boy here who has five loaves of barley bread and two fish,' he said. 'But they will not be enough for all these people.'

Jesus took the food and said a prayer. Then he asked the twelve to take some food to everyone. By a miracle, there was enough for everyone, and the leftovers filled twelve baskets!

Andrew continued to follow Jesus as he travelled from place to place, telling people about God and working many miracles of healing. The number of followers grew and grew… but so, too, did the number of enemies. The religious leaders were puzzled and angry about Jesus. Some were saying his teaching was dangerous – and wrong!

Andrew still believed that everything Jesus said and did was good and right. He and the others felt triumphant when Jesus rode a donkey into the city of Jerusalem and a great crowd welcomed Jesus as God's special king, but soon everything changed. A week later, one of the twelve turned traitor and led armed guards to arrest Jesus.

Andrew and the others were terrified. They soon heard that Jesus had been accused and condemned to death by crucifixion. Soldiers nailed him to a cross of wood and left him to die.

It seemed to the disciples that all they had believed in had come to nothing. Jesus' body was laid in a tomb and the stone door was rolled shut. Then, a few days later, some women who went to the tomb said the door was open and the body had gone.

'They're right,' Simon Peter told Andrew and the others. 'I went and saw the cloths that had been used to wrap the body. They were just lying in the tomb, neatly folded, with the cloth for the face by itself.'

That evening, when ten of the twelve were together in a locked room, Jesus appeared to them. Andrew saw the marks of the crucifixion on Jesus' body.

'As the Father sent me, so I send you,' Jesus said.

Strengthened by God's Holy Spirit, Andrew and the others were soon travelling to countries far and wide, telling people about Jesus: about how to live as friends of God, and about God's promise of new life.

On one of his journeys, Andrew went to the city of

Patras. There, he preached to the people and worked miracles. One of the people he healed was Maximilla, the wife of the local Roman ruler, Aegeates. The brother of Aegeates, Stratoklis, was impressed. 'I want to be a follower of Jesus,' he declared.

Andrew was delighted. He soon discovered that Stratoklis was wise and thoughtful.

'And I want you to be the leader of the Christians in this city,' Andrew said.

Aegeates himself was worried. 'The law says people should worship the emperor.' he said. 'I must stop people worshipping Jesus.'

Aegeates had Andrew crucified upside down on an X-shaped cross. 'Tie him on with rope,' he ordered. 'Do not nail him: make him suffer longer.'

Andrew's friends wept to see him there.

'Do not be sad,' said Andrew. 'I can only see the sky, and the sight encourages me to look forward to heaven.'

When Aegeates saw how deep Andrew's faith was, he wanted to rescue him.

'I shall be happy if you become a Christian,' replied Andrew, 'but it is time for me to die.'

No one could undo the knots that bound Andrew to the cross. Then it seemed that a light from heaven shone all around Andrew, and he died.

A Prayer in Honour of Saint Andrew

*D*ear God,

As Andrew recognized that he must follow

Jesus, may we follow what is good and right.

As Andrew kept his faith in time of trouble,

may we not let evil defeat us.

Holy Remains

Andrew's body was buried in Patras, where he died. In 357, not long after the Roman emperor Constantine became a Christian and made Christianity the official religion of his empire, Andrew's remains were taken to the great church building in Constantinople, also known as Byzantium. It was a place where, hundreds of years earlier, it was believed that Andrew had first brought the news about Jesus. Andrew became the principal saint of the place and, indeed, of all the churches beyond it to the east – in what was to become Russia.

Not long after, a monk named Regulus (sometimes called Rule) had a dream. An angel told him to take the remains of Andrew to a far corner of the world to keep them safe. The angel promised that Andrew would keep Regulus safe as he spread the news about Jesus.

An old tradition says that Regulus was allowed to take some of Andrew's remains on his travels. He finally landed in Scotland. On the rugged east coast he set up a monastery. The place where it stood is now called St Andrews. It is a little fishing port – a suitable haven for the fisherman disciple.

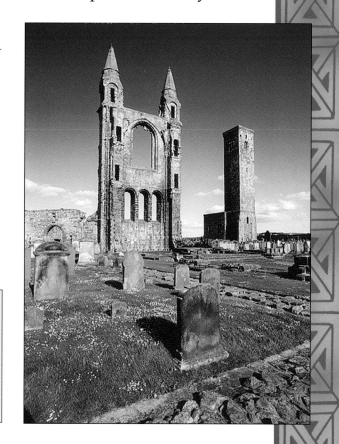

Here are the ruins of the cathedral at St Andrews. The square tower is St Regulus's Tower.

The Sign of Saint Andrew

Saint Andrew is said to have been martyred on an X-shaped cross, called the Saltire cross.

Among the old Scottish writings is a tale of a time when two Scottish peoples, the Picts and the Scots, were at war with the Angles in Northumbria. The army of the Northumbrian king, Athelstan, was far stronger. The Pictish king, Angus, prayed to God and the saints for help.

Next day, the sign of a white saltire was seen against the blue sky. The Picts and Scots were so encouraged that they won the battle.

A Pictish carving
of Pictish soldiers.

19

Saint Andrew's Day

Over the years, Saint Andrew has become an important symbol for Scotland. In 1314, after Scotland's Robert the Bruce had defeated his English enemies at Bannockburn, he declared Saint Andrew the patron saint of his country. In 1385, the Saltire cross on a blue background became the national flag of Scotland. The flag is used throughout Scotland now as a sign of all things Scottish.

In 1687, King James VII of Scotland restored the Order of Saint Andrew, also known as the Most Ancient and Most Noble Order of the Thistle. It is an exclusive order of knighthood of the United Kingdom, with membership restricted to the king or queen and sixteen others. Members of the order may wear a two-sided badge with Saint Andrew bearing his cross on one side, and a thistle on a green field on the other. The thistle has been a symbol of Scottish pride and honour for centuries.

Andrew is still remembered in churches in Scotland and around the world on his day, 30 November. Saint Andrew's Societies in many countries celebrate the day with a dinner of Scottish foods, whisky, and lively ceilidhs where bagpipes are played.

Many old traditions are linked with the day. One is that young women should listen out for barking dogs on Saint Andrew's Eve – their future husbands will come from the direction of the sound!

Scottish bagpipes are played to celebrate Saint Andrew's Day.

Index

Text by Lois Rock
Illustrations copyright © 2005 Finola Stack
This edition copyright © 2005 Lion Hudson

The moral rights of the author and illustrator
have been asserted

A Lion Children's Book
an imprint of
Lion Hudson plc
Mayfield House, 256 Banbury Road,
Oxford OX2 7DH, England
www.lionhudson.com
ISBN 0 7459 4808 1

First edition 2005
10 9 8 7 6 5 4 3 2 1 0

A catalogue record for this book is
available from the British Library

Typeset in 15/20 Revival565 BT
Printed and bound in Singapore

Picture Acknowledgments
Front cover: Sonia Halliday Photographs
Alamy Ltd: p. 19
Epic Scotland: pp. 17, 21
Sonia Halliday Photographs: p.5